L

Animals Helping at Work

ANN O. SQUIRE

Children's Press®
An Imprint of Scholastic Inc.
New York Toronto London Auckland Sydney
Mexico City New Delhi Hong Kong
Danbury, Connecticut

Content Consultant

Dr. Stephen S. Ditchkoff
Professor of Wildlife Sciences
Auburn University
Auburn, Alabama

Library of Congress Cataloging-in-Publication Data
Squire, Ann, author.
  Animals helping at work / by Ann O. Squire.
     pages cm. — (A true book)
  Summary: "Learn how animals can be trained to assist people with a variety of different jobs." —
Provided by publisher.
  Audience: Ages 9–12.
  Audience: Grades 4 to 6.
  Includes bibliographical references and index.
  ISBN 978-0-531-20509-9 (library binding : alk. paper) — ISBN 978-0-531-20535-8 (pbk. : alk. paper)
1. Working animals—Juvenile literature. 2. Animal training—Juvenile literature. 3. Animals in police
work—Juvenile literature. 4. Animals—War use—Juvenile literature. I. Title. II. Series: True book.
  SF172.S68 2015
  636.088'6—dc23   2014030575

© 2015 Scholastic Inc.
All rights reserved. Published in 2015 by Children's Press, an imprint of Scholastic Inc.
Published simultaneously in Canada. Printed in China 62
SCHOLASTIC, CHILDREN'S PRESS, A TRUE BOOK™, and associated logos are trademarks and/
or registered trademarks of Scholastic Inc.
1 2 3 4 5 6 7 8 9 10 R 24 23 22 21 20 19 18 17 16 15

Front cover: A sheepdog feeding a lamb

**Back cover: An elephant
carrying a tree branch**

Find the Truth!

Everything you are about to read is true *except* for one of the sentences on this page.

Which one is **TRUE**?

T or F Elephants, rats, and marine mammals are some of the animals that help humans.

T or F Any breed of dog can become a police dog.

Find the answers in this book.

Contents

THE BIG TRUTH!

⬅ The Iditarod Trail Sled Dog
Race is run annually in
March from Anchorage to
Nome in Alaska.

A seal collects data from the ocean's depths with a transmitter.

Mules are good at
carrying heavy loads.

Domestic house pets
spend most of their
time relaxing.

CHAPTER 1

Animals at Work

In most families, everyone has a job. Your mom and dad may go to work every day. Your job is to go to school. You might also have other tasks around the house, such as setting the table for dinner or keeping your room clean. But there are some family members who probably don't do very much at all: your pets. If you watched your pet all day, you might notice that it doesn't do anything except eat, sleep, and play!

Some animals help humans by just being companions.

Helping Out Humans

While your dog or cat spends the day relaxing, there are many other animals that go to work every day. These animal helpers assist humans in a variety of ways. Some are so strong that they can help people carry heavy loads. Others help by going places that humans can't reach. And many animals use their sharp senses of sight, smell, or hearing to help their human partners get jobs done.

Some dogs travel to distant countries as part of military operations.

8

Dogs herd sheep by rounding them up into larger groups so they don't get too spread out.

Humans' Best Friends

Dogs have been working alongside humans for thousands of years. They have guarded people, property, and livestock. Some have specialized in herding sheep and cattle. Others have been hunting companions, retrieving game and chasing after small animals in underground tunnels. Some large, strong breeds are good at pulling sleds or hauling loads. Others are trained to find missing people or to sniff out drugs or bombs.

Police dogs are also used in jails as guards and to break up fights among inmates.

Guards use dogs to help them search for phones, drugs, and other items that are against the rules in prisons.

Canine Cops

Because of their strength, intelligence, and sharp senses, dogs are employed by police departments around the world. Large breeds such as German shepherds and Belgian Malinois help fight crime and protect their human partners. These dogs are stronger and faster than most people. They can easily catch a suspect and hold him until a human police officer arrives on the scene.

Police Dog Training

Naturally aggressive breeds make the best police dogs. However, these breeds can be hard to control. For this reason, all police dogs go through obedience training. A police dog must obey its partner's commands at all times. It should be the police officer, not the dog, who decides how much force to use on a suspect.

Trainers wear special padding so they don't get hurt as dogs practice biting their targets.

Drugs, Bombs, and Bodies

A dog's sense of smell is 10,000 to 100,000 times stronger than a human's. This makes dogs perfect for sniffing out things criminals want to hide. Bloodhounds are the superstars of tracking dogs. They are often used to find missing people and escaped convicts. As a bloodhound sniffs along the ground, its large, flapping ears help fan odors up to its nose.

Bloodhounds sniff items that were touched by a victim or criminal so they will know which scent to track.

12

Izzy examines luggage for suspicious odors.

Keeping Travelers Safe

At busy airports around the world, dogs help
scan luggage for illegal items such as drugs and
weapons. They also search for things like plants
and fruit. These items may seem harmless, but they
could carry insects that might spread to a country's
crops. Izzy is a beagle who works at New York City's
Kennedy Airport. She is a passive response dog.
This means she is trained to sit down when she
detects a scent worth investigating. This prevents
her from eating the evidence!

Dogs help detect dangerous pests such as bedbugs so that workers can prevent their spread from room to room and building to building.

Sniffing Out Bedbugs

Dogs can even detect something too small to be seen by most humans: bedbugs. These tiny insects live in clothes and bedding. If there are only a small number of bedbugs or bedbug eggs, human inspectors can easily miss them. They can then spread quickly through apartment buildings. In New York City, two beagles named Mickey and Nemo have been trained to sniff out bedbugs. The dogs use their amazing sense of smell to find bedbugs or their eggs.

Finding Jack the Ripper

One of the first people to use dogs to track criminals was London police commissioner Sir Charles Warren (below) in 1889. His department was having trouble capturing a serial killer named Jack the Ripper. To help, he tried to train two dogs to follow Jack's scent from a crime scene. The results were disastrous. One of the dogs bit the commissioner, and at some point both of the dogs ran away. After that incident, police departments began using professional dog trainers.

Elephants use their long, strong trunks to pick up logs and other heavy objects.

CHAPTER 2

Strength and Stamina

Some animals are helpful to humans not because of their super senses, but because of their super strength. In many Asian countries, elephants have been used for thousands of years to carry soldiers and weapons into battle. They can also haul lumber and other heavy loads. Working elephants are still common in India, Thailand, and Myanmar (Burma). There are an estimated 15,000 to 16,000 elephants working throughout Asia today.

The elephant's great strength makes it very useful to people.

Lifting Logs

Elephants continue to play a vital role in logging in Myanmar's forests. After workers have cut down a tree, they wrap chains around it. The chains are then hooked to the elephant. The elephant drags the huge log to the nearest waterway. The log is then floated downriver to a mill. Unlike heavy machines, elephants can move logs through the forest without damaging surrounding trees.

Wading into water is no problem for an elephant.

A lifetime of hard work wears down an elephant's body.

Using elephants for logging is better for the environment than using heavy machinery, which requires roads to be cut through the forest. But the backbreaking work takes a toll on the elephants' health. After many years of hauling logs, elephants may have trouble walking. They can also develop heart conditions and other health problems. Some elephants go to retirement parks to roam and graze when they can no longer work.

Sled dogs helped soldiers travel through difficult terrain during World War I.

Sled Dogs

Before airplanes and snowmobiles, sled dogs were an essential part of life in the snow-covered wilderness. Teams of sled dogs have long been used to deliver supplies to remote areas. In the 1800s, they helped explore the Arctic and Antarctic regions. During World Wars I and II, sled dogs delivered heavy equipment and helped with rescue missions.

Sled dogs are chosen for their leadership qualities, speed, and strength. A typical sled dog weighs about 40 to 45 pounds (18 to 20 kilograms). A team of dogs can pull a load of up to 700 pounds (318 kg). This means each dog in the team may be pulling twice its own weight! Sled dogs must also be able to work in subfreezing temperatures. Most have thick, heavy coats.

Sleeping sled dogs keep warm by covering their noses with their furry tails.

Sled dogs transport a heavy load over icy tundra.

21

Balto, Hero Sled Dog

In the winter of 1925, an outbreak of diphtheria (a serious bacterial infection) threatened to sweep through the city of Nome, Alaska. The city's children faced the greatest risk of infection. A cure that could halt the outbreak existed. However, the closest supply of this medicine was in Anchorage, nearly 1,000 miles (1,609 kilometers) away. The only airplane in Anchorage that could have been used to deliver it was not working! How could the medicine possibly get to Nome in time?

Officials decided that the only way was to use sled dogs. More than 20 sled teams helped deliver the cure from Anchorage to Nome. They battled snow, ice, high winds, and temperatures well

below zero. Just six days after they left Anchorage, the final sled dog team reached Nome. They had delivered the medicine in time to stop the disease from spreading. The lead sled dog was Balto, a male Siberian husky. Balto became famous for his bravery. A year later, a bronze statue honoring him and the other sled dog teams was erected in New York City's Central Park.

An African giant pouched rat enjoys a treat after finding a land mine.

CHAPTER 3

Working Where People Cannot

In many countries around the world, buried **land mines** from long-ago wars threaten the safety of people today. Finding and disarming these mines is an extremely dangerous job. Even the smallest mistake can set off a mine. Most people do not want to risk their lives performing these tasks. Luckily, land mine detection is a perfect job for an unusual animal helper: the African giant pouched rat.

← Its keen sense of smell and small size make this rat an ideal helper.

Superb Sniffers

Giant pouched rats are larger than other types of rats. They weigh between 2 and 3.5 pounds (1 and 1.5 kg). They may be heavier than other rats, but they are still too light to set off a buried land mine. Like all rodents, pouched rats have a great sense of smell. APOPO, a nonprofit group based in Africa, trains rats to sniff out land mines that are hidden underground.

Giant pouched rats have helped find more than 2,400 land mines in Mozambique.

A rat sniffs a mine during a training exercise.

HeroRAT handlers wear protective gear to prevent injuries in case something goes wrong while the rats look for mines.

First, the rats are taught to associate the sound of a clicker device with a tasty food reward. Next, they are given different odors to smell. When they sniff at holes containing explosives, the trainer sounds the clicker and gives the rat a treat. As training progresses, the rat must search harder and harder to find the right scent. Well-trained rats learn to detect faint scents deep underground in order to earn their tasty reward.

A group of children in Thailand look at some of the explosive devices that have been uncovered near their homes.

HeroRATs

APOPO's trained rats are called HeroRATs. HeroRATs have found more than 3,700 land mines. They have also discovered bombs and ammunition. After the rats locate buried land mines, humans carefully remove the mines and deactivate them. When an area has been cleared of the explosives, the landowners are allowed to return. They can then safely plant crops or use the land as a pasture for livestock.

Marine Mammal Helpers

Another place that is difficult for humans to reach is the deep ocean. In 2006 and 2007, **climatologists** were interested in collecting data on winter water temperatures in Greenland's Baffin Bay. Winters there are harsh, though. It is impossible for researchers to cross the ice to take measurements. The solution was to hire some unusual research assistants: narwhals. The narwhal is a marine mammal with a long, spiraling tusk on its head.

A narwhal's tusk is actually a very long tooth.

The narwhal is sometimes called the unicorn of the sea.

Deep Divers

Scientists captured 14 narwhals and fitted them with temperature sensors. The sensors had transmitters that could send information back to the scientists. The animals were released. Scientists tracked their movements over three winters. The narwhals dove as deep as 5,817 feet (1,773 meters) as they searched for food in the icy waters of Baffin Bay. The data sent back by the transmitters provided new information about wintertime temperatures in the bay.

Scientists attach a device to a captured narwhal before releasing it back into the water.

A group of scientists prepares to take water samples from the depths of Baffin Bay.

Warming Waters

Unfortunately, the information collected by the narwhals confirmed what climatologists had feared. The waters of Baffin Bay are heating up. They were almost 1 degree Fahrenheit (0.55 degree Celsius) warmer than scientists had predicted. Rising water temperatures around the world are one of the effects of **global warming**. Climate change is the gradual changing of our planet's weather as a result of air pollution.

Transmitters are often attached to seals with a special type of glue.

Marine Measurements

Narwhals are just one type of marine mammal that helps humans. Seals and other deep-diving animals have been fitted with tags that measure the depth and temperature of the waters where they live and hunt. The information these animals collect is important to climate scientists, **marine biologists**, and **oceanographers**. It also helps people who are interested in fishing and tourism in the Arctic and Antarctic regions.

Pollution Problems

The former Santa Susana Field Laboratory lies just 30 miles (48 km) from Los Angeles, California. This is now one of the most toxic sites in the United States. In the 1950s, an accident at the lab released **radioactive** gases into the air. Later on, toxic chemicals were spilled onto the ground during rocket tests. Local residents fear that the area is still contaminated. The Environmental Protection Agency (EPA) uses vehicles carrying radiation detectors to sweep the area for dangerous radiation.

The equipment used to measure radiation is often very heavy.

33

Radiation-Detecting Mules

However, much of the area is too rugged and rocky for the vehicles to reach. In some places, there are **endangered** plant species that could be damaged by heavy equipment. How could the EPA do its job? With mules. These animals are sure-footed enough to reach remote areas of the hills. They do not pose a danger to plant life. And because mules are pack animals, they have the strength to carry radiation detectors and other heavy equipment.

Mules are used all around the world to carry heavy packages across difficult terrain.

A mule wears a special harness so it can carry a radiation detector.

Since radioactive material is contained in the earth and not the air, the mules are in no danger as they walk through the hills. When the detectors indicate nearby radioactivity, scientists take soil samples. They test the samples for levels of radioactivity within the soil. Then they figure out what to do next to clean the area. Once the toxic site has been cleaned up, the state of California plans to turn the land into a park.

This pigeon flew 200 miles (322 km) in five hours to deliver a message during World War I.

CHAPTER 4

Birds, Bees, and Pigs

Dogs, mules, and other mammals are not the only animals that help humans. Throughout history, birds have carried out many important jobs. They have even saved human lives. In World War I, carrier pigeons transported messages from the front battle lines back to headquarters. A pigeon named Cher Ami was one of 600 birds used by the U.S. Army Signal Corps during the war.

Carrier pigeons helped people communicate before the widespread use of radio and telephones.

A Brave Bird

Cher Ami flew missions for Major Charles Whittlesey and his men, who were stationed in France. On October 3, 1918, the American soldiers found themselves trapped behind enemy lines. They were in grave danger. Help from headquarters was the only thing that could save them. The men tried sending messages with two different pigeons, but both were shot down by enemy soldiers. Then Cher Ami took off with a note in a canister attached to his leg.

Timeline

1925
A sled team in Alaska, led by Balto, stops an outbreak of diphtheria by carrying medicine from Anchorage to Nome.

1918
The carrier pigeon Cher Ami saves 194 soldiers by delivering a message calling for help.

With bullets whizzing around him, the pigeon flew toward division headquarters 25 miles (40 km) away. Despite being shot through the chest by enemy fire, he managed to deliver the message. As a result, 194 soldiers were rescued and brought to safety. Cher Ami survived his wounds and received many military honors and awards for his service. He is one of the true animal heroes of World War I.

2006
Bees are first trained to sniff out explosives.

2003
APOPO's first land mine detection rats begin working in Mozambique.

Sniffer Bees

It's hard to imagine how bees could help humans. But like mine-sniffing rats, trained bees can respond to all kinds of scents, from gunpowder to TNT explosives. Bees are taught to associate a particular smell with a sugar water reward. When they detect a target smell, they stick out their long, hairy tongues because they expect the treat. The bees' accuracy is similar to that of a trained sniffer dog. However, bees are easier to train. They are also less expensive to care for than dogs.

A honeybee licks sugar water from a cotton swab after correctly identifying an explosive device.

Truffles are known around the world for their rich, unique flavor.

Truffles can sell for thousands of dollars per pound!

Snuffling for Truffles

You'll find truffles on the menu at some of the world's best restaurants. Truffles are a type of fungus that grows underground. They are found as deep as 3 feet (1 m) beneath the surface. Their unusual flavor makes them popular with chefs. It's not easy to find truffles, though. For centuries, people have relied on pigs to sniff them out.

Unreal Animal Helpers

Here's a surprise—animals don't have to be real to help people. Scientists around the world are designing robotic fish that look and swim just like real fish. The robots can be equipped with sensors to measure water pollution. They can also be used for underwater photography and deep-sea exploration. Robotic fish can even help scientists by swimming along with real fish and gathering information on their behavior.

Why Pigs Work Well

Why pigs? Scientists have found that truffles contain a substance that is also found in the saliva of male pigs. This substance is very attractive to female pigs. It is one of the things that bring pigs together to mate. It's no coincidence that female pigs make the best truffle hunters. The only drawback to using pigs to find truffles is that they want to gobble up every truffle they find! ★

Truffle hunters must keep a close eye on their pigs to make sure they don't eat the truffles they sniff out.

43

Number of sled dogs in a team: 4, 6, 8, 10, or unlimited

Average length of a police dog's career: 6 to 8 years

Estimated number of buried land mines in Angola: 10 million to 20 million

Area of land cleared of land mines and returned to local people in Mozambique: 2,175 acres (880 hectares)

Average flying speed of a racing carrier pigeon: 92.5 miles (149 km) per hour

Did you find the truth?

T Elephants, rats, and marine mammals are some of the animals that help humans.

F Any breed of dog can become a police dog.

Resources

Books

Goldish, Meish. *Bomb-Sniffing Dogs*. New York: Bearport Publishing, 2012.

Hoffman, Mary Ann. *Police Dogs*. New York: Gareth Stevens Publishing, 2011.

Presnall, Judith. *Carrier Pigeons*. Farmington Hills, MI: KidHaven Press, 2003.

Visit this Scholastic Web site for more information on animals helping at work:

★ www.factsfornow.scholastic.com
Enter the keywords **Animals Helping at Work**

Important Words

climatologists (klye-mi-TAH-luh-jists) — scientists who study climates and weather

endangered (en-DAYN-jurd) — in danger of becoming extinct, usually because of human activity

global warming (GLOH-buhl WARM-ing) — a warming of Earth's atmosphere and oceans that is predicted to result from an increase in the greenhouse effect caused by air pollution

land mines (LAND MYNZ) — bombs placed underground

marine biologists (muh-REEN bye-AH-luh-jists) — scientists who study fish, marine mammals, and other aquatic life

oceanographers (oh-shuh-NAH-gruh-furz) — scientists who study the ocean and the plants and animals that live in it

radioactive (ray-dee-oh-AK-tiv) — radioactive materials are made up of atoms whose nuclei break down, giving off harmful radiation

Index

Page numbers in **bold** indicate illustrations.

About the Author

Ann O. Squire is a psychologist and an animal behaviorist. Before becoming a writer, she studied the behavior of rats, tropical fish in the Caribbean, and electric fish from central Africa. Her favorite part of being a writer is the chance to learn as much as she can about all sorts of topics. In addition to the Animal Helpers books, Dr. Squire has written about many different animals, from lemmings to leopards and cicadas to cheetahs. She lives in Long Island City, New York.